Publish Great Things

Bible Modular Series

bju press®
Greenville, South Carolina

NOTE:
The fact that materials produced by other publishers may be referred to in this volume does not constitute an endorsement of the content or theological position of materials produced by such publishers. Any references and ancillary materials are listed as an aid to the student or the teacher and in an attempt to maintain the accepted academic standards of the publishing industry.

Publish Great Things

H. Douglas Garland, M.A.

Editor: Thomas Parr
Designer: Noelle Snyder
Compositor: Agnieszka Augustyniak

Greenville, South Carolina 29609

Printed in the United States of America

ISBN 978-1-60682-494-8

15 14 13 12 11 10 9 8 7 6 5

CONTENTS

Matthew 28:18-20

And Jesus came and spake unto them, saying, All power is given unto me in heaven and in earth.

Go ye therefore, and teach all nations, baptizing them in the name of the Father, and of the Son, and of the Holy Ghost:

Teaching them to observe all things whatsoever I have commanded you: and, lo, I am with you alway, even unto the end of the world. Amen.

Lord, Send Me Anywhere

O Lord, since Thou hast died
To give Thyself for me,
No sacrifice could be too great
For me to make for Thee.

I only have one life,
And that will soon be past;
I want my life to count for Christ,
What's done for Him will last.

I follow Thee, my Lord,
And glory in Thy cross;
I gladly leave the world behind
And count all gain as loss.

(chorus)
Lord, send me anywhere,
Only go with me;
Lay any burden on me,
Only sustain me.
Sever any tie,
Save the tie that binds me
To Thy heart,
Lord Jesus, my King,
I consecrate my life, Lord,
To Thee.

Introduction

At the end of history, the saints in heaven sing praise to Jesus Christ:

> *Thou art worthy to take the book,*
> *and to open the seals thereof:*
> *for thou wast slain, and hast redeemed us to God by thy blood*
> *out of every kindred, and tongue, and people, and nation;*
> *and hast made us unto our God kings and priests:*
> *and we shall reign on the earth.* (Rev. 5:9–10)

This means that one of God's purposes in history is that every people group will have at least one representative in heaven.

God wants this to happen. It will happen. God values the praises of people who aren't white, who aren't middle class, who've never used the Internet. He wants to set up third-world, dark-skinned people as rulers along with fair-haired Norwegians.

This little song, that Revelation says will be sung in the future, is a great leveler of the peoples. Every person made in God's image is valuable, and so is every nation made up of those people.

If you are a Christian, one of the future rulers of the globe, it is your privilege and responsibility to join with God in His mission to publish great things to the nations. And we already know the end of the story.

CHAPTER ONE

The Basis for Missions

1

Springtime at my house means baseball! Finding the gloves and bats, playing catch in the backyard, signing up for Little League, and listening to the Atlanta Braves point to many months of fun and competition. Several years ago the local baseball organization asked me to coach a team of seven-year-old boys. With fear and trembling, I accepted. Becoming the coach transformed me into the expert! Reading the rules of baseball proved to be the first of many humbling experiences. Although I had played organized baseball for six years, cheered as an avid fan, talked about the game and greatly enjoyed it, I soon discovered how very little I knew about the specifics of the game. This first-year coach painfully learned far more than any of the players did. The team won many games, but could have won more if the coach had known the game better.

Your involvement in the church's great missionary effort may be like my first year of coaching. I had played the game but did not know the rules. You probably often hear about missions, sometimes contribute financially, and may even know a missionary. But do you ever wonder why your pastor makes such an affair out of the annual missions conference? Why not keep all that money at the church to aid poor folks or build that new gymnasium? Why send families to places with unfamiliar names to learn a foreign language and eat strange foods when the need in this country is so great? These are good questions that deserve straight answers from our rulebook for missions, God's Word.

Though knowing the rules of baseball is necessary, I needed more to be a good coach. I had to create practice drills, organize the lineup, and motivate the team within the confines of the rules. Giving out candy bars to those who make good plays is not required by the rules, but neither is it prohibited. Candy bars helped us win and did not violate the rules, so I gave out lots of candy bars! The church today does many things related to missions that are not specifically mentioned in Scripture. Christian leaders creatively devise programs and organizations to aid in the work of missions. This book seeks to acquaint you with the rules and techniques of modern missions so that you may be an effective "team player."

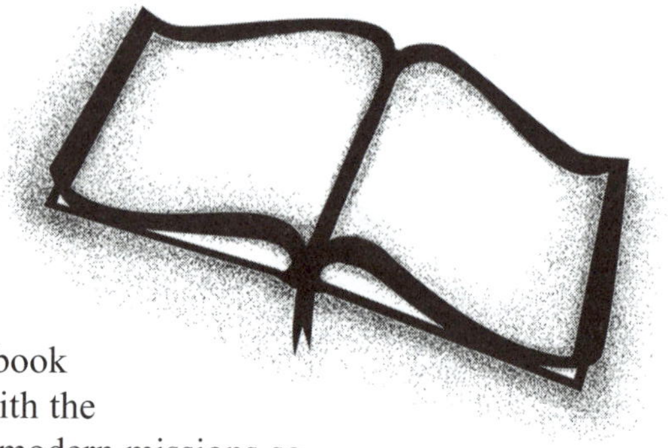

Baseball is a blast! Participating in the work of Jesus Christ around the world is much more than a "blast." It's a wonderful privilege with great reward in both time and eternity. Let's first learn the rules, and then we will discuss how you as a teen can be active in this great work.

Rules' Violations

1. In baseball, what happens when a runner leaves the baseline?
2. In soccer, what happens when a player hits the ball with his hand?
3. In basketball, what happens when a player travels with the ball?
4. In football, what happens when a player grabs a facemask?
5. In life, what happens when we don't follow God's rules?

A Look at the Rules

The best place to start learning about a complex issue is at the beginning; therefore, let's start in Genesis and work through the Old Testament. Most people are familiar with the account of Adam and Eve's creation and subsequent fall into sin. The blackness of sin provides a contrast with God that enables us to see and understand His character. God allowed Adam and Eve to eat from any tree except one. He sets boundaries around acceptable behavior for man. Adam ignored the boundary when he ate from the tree and immediately began receiving the negative consequences of his action.

In biblical studies, "death" means separation from God and has implications in both the present and the future. God expelled the first family from the Garden of Eden, and eventually Adam's body died. More importantly, Adam could no longer fellowship with God as before, and his sin infected the entire human race. The apostle Paul tells us, "Wherefore, as by one man sin entered into the world, and death by sin; and so death passed upon all men, for that all have sinned" (Rom. 5:12). Mankind's chief characteristic throughout time is not his intelligence, physical strength, or vast accomplishments, but his sinful nature. Every obituary and every cemetery should remind us of Adam's disobedience and our disobedience to a holy God.

God was not willing to leave Adam or the rest of humanity in such a hopeless condition. First, God told the serpent who enticed Eve to sin that in time a child born to the woman would gain ultimate victory over evil (Gen. 3:15). The conflict between the "seed of the woman" and evil is one of the main themes of the Bible. Second, until this final victory occurred, God made a temporary provision to restore at least part of what was lost in Adam's disobedience. This provision was "coats of skins" to clothe the first couple (Gen. 3:21). Remember that they complained about being naked and afraid. The skins covered the nakedness and also pointed to the important concept "atonement," which means "covering." The animal died in Adam's place. Notice, however, that many consequences of the sin remained, including expulsion from the Garden, and had to be faced by Adam for the rest of his life on earth.

Some of you may exclaim, "The 'rules' of missions sound a lot like a Bible doctrines class!" You are absolutely correct. All faith and practice, what we believe and do, must come directly from the Bible. Genesis is a book of foundations. The remaining 65 books develop the themes introduced in Genesis. Let's make sure we understand the basics from the account of man's fall. Man is a sinful being deserving death for his disobedience. God, however, introduced a plan to restore fellowship with man through the coming Redeemer and illustrated the plan by covering the guilty couple with coats of skins. Animals don't normally donate their skins. The coats required the death of the animal. The Lord transferred the penalty ("thou shalt surely die"—Gen. 2:17) to an innocent party in order to restore man to partial fellowship. The concepts in Genesis are at the very heart of missions today. Man rebels against God and is now subject to God's wrath. God provided for man's salvation through Jesus Christ and now seeks for the practical restoration of fellowship. In simple terms, *missions is telling other people about the saving power of Jesus Christ and the new life that follows.*

God's Missionary Heart

The Old Testament centers on God's missionary heart. Through ordinary people, eloquent prophets, righteous politicians, natural wonders, and occasional miracles, God reaches out to humanity with the message of salvation. Let's look at just a few examples.

Terms in the Field

Sin—disobedience to the will of God (Rom. 3:23)

Fall—Adam disobeyed God, resulting in his fall from a state of innocence into sin. All men now have a natural inclination toward sin.

Atonement—a covering, especially in relation to sin. The blood of a sacrifice covered the sins from God's eyes and made forgiveness possible.

Death—Spiritual death is separation from God, while physical death is a separation of the body from the soul. Both resulted as penalties for sin.

Righteousness—conformity to God's standards for life and being

Gentiles—people or nations that were not part of Israel

Word—the English translation of the Greek *logos,* which means "statement" or "thought." Jesus is God's statement to man about life. John uses *logos* to describe the eternal and human nature of Jesus Christ.

Ransom—the price paid by Christ through His death on the cross, resulting in our redemption

Salvation—the great deliverance from the guilt and the pollution of sin accomplished by Christ

---

1. Noah, the man who built the ark at God's direction, was a preacher of righteousness (II Peter 2:5). What did he preach? We do not have any of his sermons, but we can speculate based on the information that we do have. Noah preached about the effects of sin, about God's judgment, and about salvation. The ark was a huge object lesson for many years, but only his family believed. The entire world perished because the people refused the message of restoration.

Isaiah's Prophecies

A "prophet" is someone who speaks at God's direction and for God. At times, God used these men to reveal future events. Isaiah eloquently spoke of the coming Savior to the extent that many Bible students call his writings the Fifth Gospel. Can you think of some things that Isaiah's prophecies teach us about God's plans and intentions regarding salvation?

2. God called a man named Abram out of Ur of the Chaldees and gave him the land of Canaan. Part of the communication and promise to Abram was "in thee shall all the families of the earth be blessed" (Gen. 12:3). How could one man influence every family of the earth? God through His providence and sovereignty created the nation of Israel through Abram's descendants. Through the nation of Israel, God sent His Son as the promised "seed of the woman" (Gen. 3:15) to redeem mankind. Paul said in Galatians 3:14, "That the blessing of Abraham might come on the Gentiles through Jesus Christ."

3. The mighty prophet Isaiah delivered the message of God's salvation to Israel and to the world. Many of the Jews of Isaiah's time believed that being a descendant of Abraham was the primary requirement for salvation. "Though your sins be as scarlet, they shall be as white as snow" (Isa. 1:18) reminded them that sin separated man from God and that God had a plan to deal with sin. Isaiah further emphasized that God's plan was not restricted to the Jew. "I will also give thee for a light to the Gentiles, that thou mayest be my salvation unto the end of the earth" (Isa. 49:6). Isaiah 53 is perhaps one of the best-known chapters in the Old Testament. The suffering servant of the Lord pays the penalty for the people's sin and then justifies them.

*T*he Work of Christ

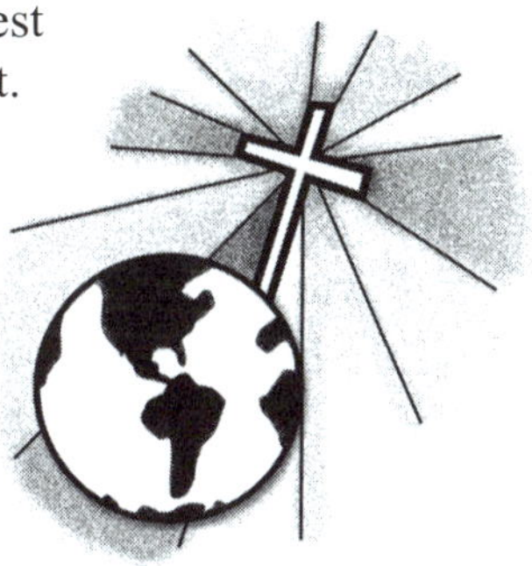

God's missionary heart reaches its highest peak in the person and work of Jesus Christ. Why did Jesus come into this sin-cursed world? Why did He die? Once again we must turn to the Scriptures for the answers. Remember that the Gospel of John identifies Christ as the Word. Language scholars debate the meaning of the term, but it generally encompasses God's specific revelation to man. The *thus saith the Lord* of the Old Testament is the incarnate Word of the New Testament.

Most of us have made orange juice from concentrate. Like little children, we may scrape the side of the can with our finger and then taste the thick liquid. The juice can be so strong that our eyes water! In a sense, Jesus Christ is God's revelation of Himself in condensed and living form. The message is powerful, sharp, and not easily forgotten. *God sent His Son to save the souls of mankind.* What are some of the specifics of the message? Let's use a chart based on John 1 to see some familiar themes (see chart on page 8).

Every aspect of Christ's life displays his zeal to save mankind from the consequences of sin. Jesus continually taught people about God. The Jews of His day practiced a religion that was a

Seeing Parts of the Whole Picture

Unbelieving scholars often acknowledge a particular aspect of Jesus' ministry, but fail to see the entire picture. Half of a baseball bat will not allow you to hit many home runs! Believing only a portion of what the Bible says about Jesus is like striking out in life! Can you discern what's missing from the following teachings about Christ?

1. Jesus was the best of all teachers.
2. Jesus was an example of how we should live.
3. Jesus was merely a man.
4. Jesus is as dead as any man in the cemetery.
5. Jesus is a way to heaven.

combination of God's truth and man's traditions. Jesus preached the Sermon on the Mount to strip away the foolish inventions of man and to show God's ways. Proverbs 16:25 says, "There is a way that seemeth right unto a man, but the end thereof are the ways of death." But Jesus' purpose extended far beyond a teaching ministry.

He came to die for the sins of mankind. "For even the Son of man came not to be ministered unto, but to minister, and to give his life a ransom for many" (Mark 10:45). Liberal theologians and unbelievers often view the death of Christ as a mistake or an

John 1 Themes

Verse	Text	Teaching	OT Reference
John 1:5	And the light shineth in darkness; and the darkness comprehended it not.	Man is sinful and therefore rejects God's goodness in Christ.	*Genesis 3* Adam sinned and broke fellowship with God.
John 1:10	The world knew him not.		
John 1:11	His own received him not.		
John 1:12	But as many as received him, to them gave he power to become the sons of God.	Salvation is through Christ.	*Genesis 3:15* "seed of the woman"
John 1:13	Which were born . . . of God.	God initiates salvation for sinners.	*Genesis 3:21* "Unto Adam also and to his wife did the Lord God make coats of skins, and clothed them."

unfortunate set of circumstances. Even a brief survey of the Gospels, however, shows that Jesus' purpose from the very beginning was to die on a cross to save sinners. John the Baptist announced, "Behold the Lamb of God, which taketh away the sin of the world" (John 1:29). Jesus told Nicodemus, "even so must the Son of man be lifted up: that whosoever believeth in him should not perish, but have eternal life" (John 3:14-15).

Jesus immediately began to call and train a group of followers who would spread the news of salvation after His return to heaven. These men were initially called disciples and later apostles. As Simon and John fished in the Sea of Galilee, Jesus enlisted them for the job of "fishing for men." For the next three years they heard Jesus' preaching, watched Him heal people, and experienced His kind and often firm rebukes. Only after Jesus' death and resurrection did they begin to understand the real intent of their training. Jesus prepared them to spread the news of salvation from sin. Some of Christ's last words on the earth we know as the Great Commission. "Go ye therefore and teach all nations" (Matt. 28:19) was now the guiding principle for those who believed in Jesus Christ. The Book of Acts records how they spread the gospel to the world.

MATERIAL FOR THE MIND

Are You a Mission Field?

Let's think about something together. If Jesus died to take away the sins of the world, have your sins been taken away? The best baseball glove in the world will not help you play the game unless you put it on and use it. Jesus' work and offer of salvation will likewise not save you unless you put it on. It's not hard! All we do is ask Jesus to save us and believe that He does! Remember what Jesus said to Nicodemus in John 3:15? "Whosoever believeth in him should not perish, but have eternal life." Ask your teacher or pastor for additional help.

Review Questions

True or False

F 1. God created death as the natural end of life.

F 2. Missions is only a New Testament concept.

T 3. God blesses believers today in connection with a promise made to Abraham.

T 4. Faith is required for salvation.

F 5. The Sermon on the Mount rebukes religious error.

Matching

Choose the best answer from the list for each item.

A. Proclaiming Christ
B. Deliverance from sin
C. Disobedience
D. Self-worth
E. Ability to know the facts
F. Conformity to God's ways
G. Price of redemption
H. Separation from God

F 6. Righteousness

____ 7. Ransom

____ 8. Missions

____ 9. Sin

____ 10. Salvation

Essay

Write one or two complete sentences to answer each item.

11. Explain why understanding the rules and theory of missions is important.

12. God records similar ideas in both the Old and the New Testaments. Suggest what this teaches us about God and what impact it has on believers today.

13. Develop the idea that Noah's ark was an object lesson about salvation.

Short Answer

15. What is the primary rule of missions for the modern church?

16. Where do we find the rule?

Chapter Two

Spreading the News!

2

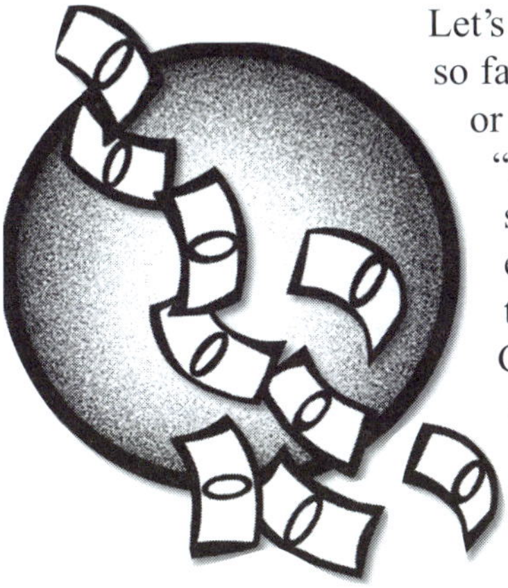

Let's think about what we have learned so far. Missions begins with theology, or the study of God. The great "rule" of missions is that God desires fellowship with man. All the events of the Old Testament point to the coming of Jesus Christ, God's Son, who would die to take away the sins of mankind. Jesus trained His disciples and commissioned them to go into the entire world spreading the news of salvation.

Great principles or rules govern every aspect of our lives. The banking industry depends in part upon mathematics to keep your financial accounts in order. Imagine that you deposited $50 into a $500 savings account. The bank now shows that you have $550. What would you say if after adding the $50, the bank registered that you had $400? Likewise, the principles of mathematics govern the building industry. An engineer calculates that a wooden beam of a certain size will hold up the weight of your house and all of its contents. The computation required for the

MATERIAL FOR THE MIND

Guiding Principles

Basic principles guide every occupation and enterprise of man. What academic fields would a student study to enter the following occupations?

Medicine:
Journalism:
Air travel:
Government:
Farming:

beam selection means that you will not fall through the floor while you sleep at night!

God's great desire to fellowship with man should therefore be the guiding principle for believers today. In this chapter we will study how the early church applied the principle, and we will formulate some corollaries for mission activities today. Remember, a corollary is a naturally drawn conclusion from an accepted truth. Once we know the "rules" and how to apply them, we will be ready to start working on the skills of missions.

The First Missionaries

The last words of men often provoke emotion, thought, and action. Just prior to being hanged by the British as a spy during the American Revolutionary War, Nathan Hale said, "I only regret I have but one life to lose for my country." His words motivated George Washington's army to fight the war with great passion. Captain Hale's words still inspire those fighting for country and principle today. Jesus Christ, just before returning to heaven, gave His disciples a very straightforward command.

> It is not for you to know the times or the seasons, which the Father hath put in his own power. But ye shall receive power, after that the Holy Ghost is come upon you: and ye shall be witnesses unto me both in Jerusalem, and in all Judaea, and in Samaria, and unto the uttermost part of the earth (Acts 1:7-8).

Christ's words form the very backbone of the Book of Acts and of the first missionary effort. Let's examine these verses carefully. Notice that all three members of the Trinity actively participate in the work. God the Father directs the work of redemption but does not reveal the specific times of important events. Jesus Christ the Son communicates God's will to the apostles and is the subject of the

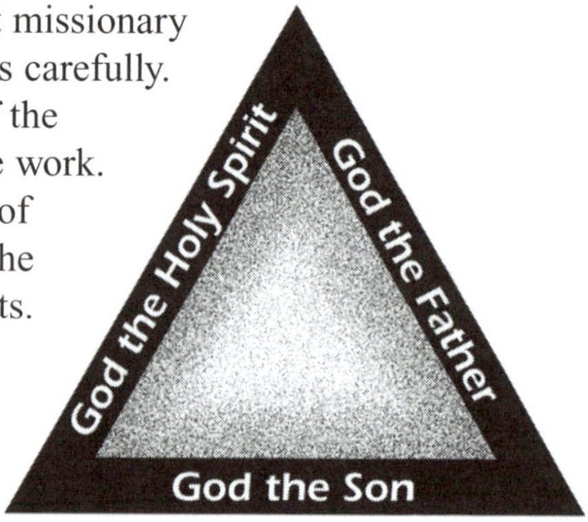

The Structure of Acts

An outline is an organized presentation of the major events in a book of history. Outlines help us understand how the various events and chapters fit together. As you read the Book of Acts, use the following outline to focus on the main teachings of the book.

I. Spreading the Gospel in Jerusalem, Acts 1-7
II. Spreading the Gospel in Judea and Samaria, Acts 8-12
III. Spreading the Gospel to the World, Acts 13-28

---

apostles' proclamation. The Holy Spirit empowers the messengers and the message.

Put yourself in the place of the apostles. They knew that Jesus was God. His resurrection from the dead removed all doubt. The way of salvation was clearly through Christ. What should they do now? Jesus' words became their marching orders. Trust that God controls the events of life. Wait for the power of the Holy Spirit and then witness for Jesus Christ both at home and around the world.

Military commanders expect soldiers to obey orders. Your parents probably expect you to do certain chores and to participate in church and school activities. God likewise fully expected the apostles to perform His will. An examination of the Book of Acts shows that the apostles did exactly as Christ commanded. The apostles and other believers returned to Jerusalem to pray and to wait for the coming of the Holy Spirit. On the day of Pentecost, God sent the Holy Spirit to fill or to dwell within the believers. Since the Holy Spirit could not be seen, the believers needed a tangible indication of the Spirit's presence. Each believer heard a mighty wind, saw fire, and then miraculously began to speak in foreign languages. People visiting Jerusalem for Pentecost heard the apostles speaking in many different languages. Peter used the occasion to preach an eloquent sermon on the life and work of Jesus Christ. Some three thousand people believed on Christ and joined in fellowship with the apostles.

For a few years the believers stayed in Jerusalem as God began a new organization that we know as the church. The apostles viewed Jesus Christ and the gift of the Holy Spirit as the fulfillment of God's promises in the Old Testament. Staying near the temple and the worship activities seemed natural. The Jewish leaders who had crucified Jesus began persecuting the new believers in an attempt to destroy what they saw as a false religion. Saul of Tarsus zealously sought to eliminate the early Christians, but God used this wicked man to further spread the gospel. God instructed the apostles to preach Christ everywhere. Saul's actions caused the believers to scatter into Judea and Samaria with the news of Christ. A short time later, Saul traveled to Damascus looking for believers in order to bring them back to Jerusalem for punishment. Jesus Himself met Saul on the road, and Saul trusted Christ as his Savior. The Jews likewise persecuted Saul for his new faith.

In the early years of the church, the believers preached Christ to the Jews only. Before going back to heaven, Jesus told them to preach "unto the uttermost part of the earth." Jesus' words seemed to indicate that the non-Jewish world should hear the gospel as well. One day the apostle Peter saw a strange vision, and then some Gentile men asked him to come and preach the truth to them. Peter preached Christ, the people believed, and the Holy Spirit filled the new believers. The church at Jerusalem called for Peter to explain his actions, since dealing with the Gentiles was something new. Eventually all concluded that God wanted to save both Jews and Gentiles.

Barnabas and Saul spent much time in Antioch establishing a church. The Holy Spirit spoke to the leaders and directed them to send Barnabas and Saul on a trip to establish additional churches. This was Saul's (Paul's) first missionary journey. Two more trips would follow. God used Paul to preach Christ to most of the Roman world. Some places gladly received the news of salvation. Others rejected it. The unbelieving Jews in

Jerusalem tried to destroy Paul, but he used his Roman citizenship to appeal to Caesar for deliverance. The Book of Acts ends with Paul preaching the gospel while under house arrest in Rome. The government later beheaded Paul for his preaching about Christ.

Learning from Acts

Luke, the author of Acts, records the activities of key people and events for the first thirty years of the early church. One book cannot possibly contain every single event. We believe that Luke wrote by the inspiration of the Holy Spirit. Luke's words and thoughts were actually the words that God wanted him to write for us. God expects us to know what happened as the believers spread the news of Christ. The events of Acts should teach us principles about God and how we should spread the gospel today. Remember the "rule" of missions? God wants fellowship with man through Jesus Christ. Let's now look at some of the corollaries, or conclusions, about missions that we see in the Book of Acts.

First, the Holy Spirit guided the early church's effort to evangelize the world. The Spirit filled Peter on the day of Pentecost and three thousand came to Christ. Officers in the church had to be filled with the Spirit. Stephen, the first man to die for Christ, testified to the Jewish leaders through the power of the Spirit. The work to the Gentiles began when the Holy Spirit spoke to Peter about preaching to Cornelius. The work continued when the Spirit separated Barnabas and Saul for the first missionary journey. Eventually, Paul wanted to go into Asia, but the Spirit directed him to Macedonia.

Second, the main task of the first missionaries was to preach Jesus Christ. *Ye shall be witnesses unto me* were Jesus' commanding words. Peter boldly proclaimed in the temple that the Jewish

The Life of Paul the Apostle

God greatly used the apostle Paul in many different situations and places. Find one or more places in Acts that illustrate the following characteristics of Paul's life:

- Preached Christ publicly
- Used the Old Testament Scriptures
- Defended his faith in Christ
- Traveled extensively
- Knew the culture of the Roman Empire
- Spoke various languages
- Endured hardship or persecution

leaders killed Christ but that God raised Him from the dead. Philip explained references to Jesus in the book of Isaiah to an Ethiopian eunuch. Shortly after being saved, Saul proclaimed Christ in the synagogue at Damascus. Peter preached Christ to Cornelius. In every city, Paul and his companions explained the life and work of Christ to both Jews and Gentiles. Some believed the Word of God and others rejected it.

Third, the apostles and other leaders established local churches to help the new believers grow in faith. Unbelieving Jews often expelled the new Christians from the synagogues. The believers then began meeting in houses to worship God and to hear His Word. In time, the church at Jerusalem established a congregation at Antioch that became the base of operations for Paul's three missionary journeys. Paul and his companions visited many cities, preached the gospel, and established churches throughout the Roman world. He later wrote to the churches that he was unable to revisit. Many needed encouragement to continue spiritual growth. Others faced serious persecution and problems. Paul's letters comprise much of our New Testament.

Fourth, early missionaries often helped people with physical needs. Peter healed a crippled man in the temple. The people saw what happened and were then eager to hear what Peter had to say about Jesus. Part of Philip's ministry in Samaria included casting out demons and healing physical maladies, which led to preaching opportunities. Acts 9:35 tells us that all the people in Lydda and Saron trusted Christ after they knew that Peter had healed a man with palsy. Paul healed a crippled man at Lystra and the people believed that he was a god. Paul then preached Christ to them. As Paul traveled to Rome, he healed Publius' father, among others. Many people listened to God's Word when they saw the compassion of the early Christians. Meeting physical needs was not the goal but simply a tool to gain the people's attention and acceptance.

Fifth, the early church regularly defended the faith and endured persecution. Stephen did both and lost his life for Christ's sake. Herod killed James the brother of John and tried to kill Peter as well. An angel delivered Peter from prison. The Jews followed Paul from city to city trying to stop his preaching. At Jerusalem, Paul made several long speeches to the Jews and to government officials about his faith in Christ and the work that God was doing. The Jews viewed faith in Christ as heresy. Rome looked at Christianity as a threat to the government religion. Both tried to destroy the work of Christ. God's authority over the actions of men protected the young church. The persecution also aided the believers in spreading the Word unto the uttermost part of the earth.

Sixth, the new missionaries frequently reported on the work to the main churches at Jerusalem and Antioch. Peter and John endured the criticism of the Jewish religious leaders in Jerusalem and then recounted the events to the church. Peter also had to explain his actions and the conversion of Cornelius to the church. At the

---

Living for God in Pagan Society

Traveling from Jerusalem to Rome takes about 4 hours on a modern jet. In Paul's time, the same trip took months via a Roman ship or boat that often carried prisoners, animals, and cargo. The physical hardships of life were insignificant compared to the pressures of living for God in a place that did not know or respect God. Look in a textbook, encyclopedia, or on the Internet for clues about the spiritual pressures that Paul and other Christians faced in the first-century Roman world. How is the ancient Roman world similar to society today?

end of the first missionary journey, Paul gathered the church together and "rehearsed all that God had done with them, and how he [God] had opened the door of faith unto the Gentiles" (Acts 14:27). He also reminded the Ephesian leaders of his ministry to them.

Today

The early church worked hard to obey Jesus' command to spread the news of salvation over the entire world. Most Christian leaders in Acts not only lived to proclaim Jesus, they died for proclaiming Jesus. Let's consider how their obedience and action affect us today.

One of my favorite track and field sports is the 4 × 100 relay race. Each team has four runners. The first runner sprints down the track and hands a baton to the next person, who hands it to the next person. Finally, the last runner takes the baton and dashes across the finish line. To win, everyone must focus on the same goal and carry the same baton at the appropriate time. The early church reached much of the Roman world with the gospel of Christ and gave future generations the principles to continue the race. The baton is now in our hands. What will we do with the message of Jesus Christ? Now that we know the rules and the principles, we need to begin thinking about how we will carry the news of Jesus Christ to our world.

Terms in the Field

Theology—the study of God.

Disciple—a follower of a teacher or master.

Trinity—the three coequal and coeternal persons of the Godhead: God the Father; God the Son; God the Holy Spirit.

Holy Ghost—the old English term for the third member of the Trinity, God the Holy Spirit.

Pentecost—a Jewish festival of harvest beginning seven weeks from the Passover observance. God gave the Holy Spirit to the believers on the day of Pentecost in Acts 2.

Jews—the descendants of Abraham, Isaac, and Jacob that formed the nation of Israel.

Gentiles—non-Jewish people of the world.

Pagans—a broad term denoting those who do not know the one true God.

Persecute—to harass, mistreat, or punish.

Gospel—"good news," the term that refers to the Christian message of salvation.

Evangelize—to announce the good news of the gospel.

Missionary—a person sent to preach the gospel.

Inspiration—the supernatural influence exerted on the authors of the Bible by the Holy Spirit. Inspiration gives the writings divine authority and trustworthiness.

Review Questions

Short Answer

1. To what four places did Christ command the apostles to witness?

2. When did the Holy Spirit first fill the believers?

3. Who established the church at Antioch?

4. What Old Testament book did Philip use when speaking to the Ethiopian eunuch?

5. What government official tried to kill Peter?

True or False

_____ 6. The great principle of missions is God's desire to establish local churches.

_____ 7. The Book of Acts ends with Paul under house arrest in Rome.

_____ 8. Jews gladly welcomed new Christians into the synagogues.

_____ 9. Paul made five missionary journeys.

_____ 10. The Roman government tried to destroy Christians.

CHAPTER THREE

Missions Today

3

James Naismith's job was to invent a new winter game that would keep the attention of eighteen particularly difficult students. The game needed lots of physical activity, simple rules, and it had to be played indoors. Other instructors had failed before him. In fact, Mr. Naismith's first attempts at a new game also failed. He then combined the concepts of American football and lacrosse to form thirteen rules for the new game. In December of 1891, his students read the rules and began playing the first basketball game. By 1936, basketball's popularity had so captured the attention of sports enthusiasts that it became part of the Winter Olympics. James Naismith understood the needs of his students and created the means to meet the needs.

Modern basketball coaches may not invent the rules of the game, but they still must understand the players and adapt a strategy for winning. Have you ever noticed a sports coach standing away from his players and just watching them? What is he doing? The coach is simply evaluating the strengths and weaknesses of his team before adopting a plan for the game. Likewise, evaluating a gym or an arena may reveal a small fact that will help the team to win. The coach may tell the players to sit on one side of the bench away from an electric fan in order to avoid muscle cramps. Victory depends upon keeping the rules and upon using the players in the best possible way.

Modern missions is much the same as coaching a basketball team. God gave His people a set of rules for spreading the news of salvation. Our task is to understand the rules and to apply them to the current world situation. Today, we also have the advantage of examining how the early church applied the rules and principles. Changing the rules is not our job. Rather, we need to evaluate the world around us and then formulate a strategy for proclaiming the gospel of Christ to every person. *Go ye into all the world* is Jesus' command for us today! Missions takes God's desires and rules and then applies them to the world situation. Let's look at how it works.

The Court for Missions

A basketball coach knows that the actual floor or court is 84' by 50' for high school. Each team may have five players on the court for the game. A smart coach knows who plays for the other team, how good they are, and how well they play together. In fact, a coach may go to other teams' games just to watch and learn.

How big is the court for missions? The amount of land on the earth has not changed much in the last 4,000 years. Scientists believe that the earth has about 58,000,000 square miles of land compared to 130,000,000 square miles of water. The land stays about the same, but the number of people continues to increase. Notice in the chart that the general population is increasing at about twice the rate of Christians. Also, the term "Christian" may denote family affiliation or cultural tradition and not necessarily those who truly know Christ as personal Savior. Therefore, the number of converted Christians is much smaller than shown. The sum total of people who have never heard the gospel remains the same today as it was in 1970 *(International Bulletin of Missionary Research,* Jan. 1999, p. 24). What does the

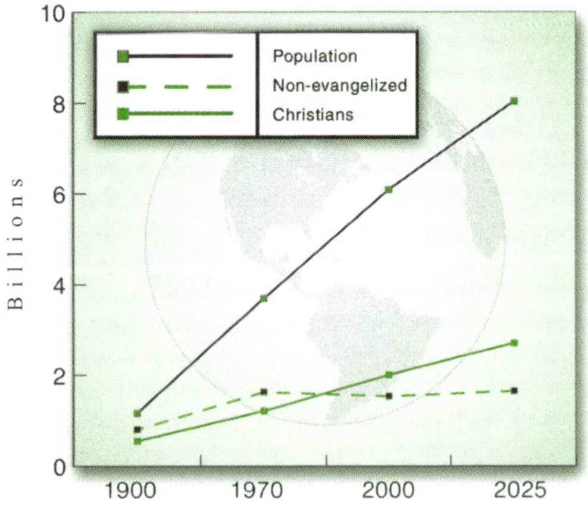

chart teach us? The opportunity for missions is huge! More people are hearing the gospel but fewer are becoming Christians.

Just as a basketball team is divided into specific positions, so the people of the world are divided into races, countries, and language groups. Scholars identify over 10,000 people groups based on differing cultures and languages. The academic field of anthropology seeks to study man's diverse physical and cultural traits. Biblical anthropology seeks to understand man and society according to the teachings of the Bible.

The world also contains some 200-250 political divisions or countries. Open countries accept foreign missionaries, while closed countries exclude missionaries. In recent years, religions hostile to Christianity increasingly dominated many countries between the 10th and 40th north latitude lines (the 10-40 window), which includes North Africa and most of southern Asia. These areas continue to grow in population, power, and influence.

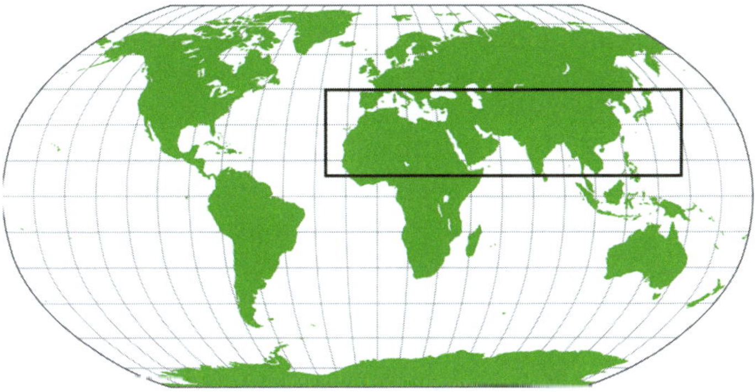

Understanding the Need

World population exceeded six billion in the year 2000. Grasping huge numbers is often easier when we use something with which we know to make a comparison. One new U.S. penny is 0.0610235 inches thick. Find the population of the following places, and calculate the height of a stack of pennies if each penny represents one person.

1. Your class
2. Your school
3. State
4. Country
5. Hometown
6. World

*U*nderstanding the Game

If you have ever traveled to another country, you know that the people and their lifestyles can be very different from what you are used to. Understanding the world's enormous population, the political systems, and philosophies (along with the differing cultures) is beyond the capacity of any one person. As Christians, we should examine the teaching of God's Word as we seek to understand the complexities of mankind.

God created man in His own image. Scholars debate the specific meaning of *image,* but most agree it means that man is separate from animals and can fellowship with God. Man rebelled against God through disobedience, which disrupted man's fellowship and corrupted the entire race. The apostle Paul eloquently describes the history and present condition of mankind in Romans 1:21-25:

> Because that, when they knew God, they glorified him not as God, neither were thankful; but became vain in their imaginations, and their foolish heart was darkened. Professing themselves to be wise, they became fools, And changed the glory of the uncorruptible God into an image made like to corruptible man, and to birds, and fourfooted beasts, and creeping things. Wherefore God also gave them up to uncleanness through the lusts of their own hearts, to dishonour their own bodies between themselves: Who changed the truth of God into a lie, and worshipped and served the creature more than the Creator, who is blessed for ever. Amen.

Even more frightening than man's sinfulness in life is the prospect of God's eternal judgment. Hebrew 9:27 says, "And as it is appointed unto men once to die, but after this the judgment." Christ himself spoke often on the agonies of hell. The Bible clearly describes God's final evaluation of and judgment

Grasping the Grammar

The basic English sentence consists of a subject, a verb, and an object. Writers often add interest and variety by changing the order of a sentence or omitting certain parts. Analyze Romans 1:21-25 and try to reconstruct the basic subject-verb-object sentence pattern. Notice man's increasing separation from God. Can you see the results of man's sin by reading a newspaper or an encyclopedia?

---

upon mankind. The sinful men that failed in life to acknowledge God's plan for salvation are cast into the lake of fire for eternity (Rev. 20:11-15).

The Bible's description of man is sobering. Humanity's common threads of sin and the need for salvation can be seen in every nation, language group, and culture. Billions of people never hear about Jesus Christ. Others hear about Jesus but choose to reject Him. God's judgment looms in the future. One day Jesus confronted a sinful woman with the eternal truths of judgment and salvation. His disciples wondered why He even bothered to speak to her. Jesus rebuked them by revealing His attitude about sinners: "Say not ye, There are yet four months, and then cometh harvest? behold, I say unto you, Lift up your eyes, and look on the fields; for they are white already to harvest" (John 4:35). Christians need to see the world as a gigantic harvest field of souls!

The Home Team

Missionaries are people just like you and me. They understand the needs of the world. God calls them to go and to reach others for Christ. On a school basketball team, the number of players is limited, and often the coach holds tryouts to determine exactly who makes the team and who does not. Many talented players never make the team, but they still play the game in other places. You may even have a hoop in your driveway or neighborhood park. The point is that God may not call you to go as a full-time missionary to Africa or South America. You can still participate in the "game" of reaching lost people for Christ in your hometown and in your neighborhood. Remember Christ's final admonition to the disciples in Acts 1:8? Jerusalem was their hometown, Judea was the county or province, and Samaria was the next closest country. People everywhere need the gospel, and you certainly can do your part whether it's near or in a faraway place. Welcome to the team!

> Ye shall be witnesses unto me both in Jerusalem, and in all Judaea, and in Samaria, and unto the uttermost part of the earth (Acts 1:8).

The Support Staff

Many people manage the functions that support an organized basketball team. Some arrange transportation, others provide meals or wash the uniforms. Somebody needs to collect the money and pay the bills. The missionary effort today requires a support staff too.

Let's first think about the church's relationship to missions. The church is not a physical building; it is a group of people called out of the world system to know and serve God. Jesus Christ established and empowered the church to proclaim the gospel to the whole world. In Matthew 16:18, the recognition of Christ's deity is the foundation for the church's existence and success. Jesus said, "I will build my church; and the gates of hell shall not prevail against it." The Greek word translated *build* is often used in other passages for the construction of a house or a structure.

What is your home used for? Most would answer that a home is used for meals, sleeping, family activities, and shelter. Our lives revolve around the home. Missions should therefore revolve around and proceed from the church. Notice also that the forces of evil will not overcome the church. "Gates" in the ancient world were places of government and authority. The decrees and actions of the Roman Empire or future human regimes would not thwart the church's evangelistic effort and growth.

Jesus also gave the church the authority to manage the affairs of the kingdom of God on earth (Matt. 16:19). If you have the key to your car, you have the authority to drive and use the car. Your friend who does not have the key cannot drive your car. Having a key does not, however, give you the right to break the law. The church therefore has the power to make decisions about the ministry within the guiding principles established in the Word of God.

Another important passage concerning the church's missionary function is Acts 13. Saul (Paul) and Barnabas taught the new believers in Antioch for about a year. God's blessing included many conversions to Christ, the establishment of a vibrant testimony, and the demonstration of compassion for the physical needs of other believers (Acts 11:22-30). One day as the work progressed, the Holy Spirit revealed that the church should send out Barnabas and Saul to preach in other places. After the church prayed and fasted, the men departed for what would become three distinct

Considering the Difference

Jason and his family will be going to Manaus, Brazil on the Amazon River. His father will teach at a Bible college while his mother cares for the family. About twenty churches send money to support them. Jason just finished reading Acts. He begins thinking about how his missionary experience will be different from the Apostle Paul's. Use an encyclopedia or the Internet to learn about Brazil. How will Jason's life be different from Paul's?

missionary journeys. Matthew 16 gives us the principle of the church's authority and power. Acts 13 shows us in part the practical outworking of the church's power. The church at Antioch sent out the first missionaries and supported them through the years.

Life has changed in many ways from the first century, but God's plan for the church remains the same. The local church should be sending out people to win the lost both in the community and around the world. Paul did not need very much to travel and to live in the Roman world. Modern missionaries may need housing, transportation, food, supplies and many other things, depending upon their ministry and location. Remember that times and needs may change, but God's blueprint remains the same. The church should therefore actively provide whatever a missionary needs to accomplish the work.

Mission Boards

Many years ago, church leaders realized that most local churches did not have the expertise to provide for the needs and support of foreign missionaries. At the same time, the leadership wanted to follow the Bible's teaching that the church should be sending out and aiding Christian workers around the world. Groups of churches then loosely banded themselves together and formed a new organization known as the mission board. Your local church probably supports missionaries through one or more mission boards.

The Bible discusses the church in many places. The mission board is a modern invention and is not mentioned in the

Scriptures. Remembering that as Christians, we need to base everything we do upon the Word of God, let's think about whether or not we should have mission boards. Christ empowered the church in Matthew 16 to make decisions about the ministry. Acts 6 records a church decision about the care of widows. The apostles were neglecting the preaching of the Word in order to provide for the ladies. They decided to formulate a new entity or position that we know as deacons and give them the responsibility for the physical care of the widows. The church selected spiritually-minded men for the new job, and the ministry prospered as a result. Paul, in the book of I Timothy, gives us a list of qualifications for deacons. Since Paul was writing under the guidance and inspiration of the Holy Spirit, we know that the office of deacon was God's will. Keep in mind that the church created the office of deacon.

Centuries later, the church created mission boards to meet similar needs. Managing the routine affairs of a missionary or groups of missionaries would drain the local church of the time and energy required to preach the Word of God. The church may therefore delegate the administrative responsibility of missions to the mission board.

Mission boards today perform several vital tasks for missionaries and local churches. Supplying all the financial and physical needs of a missionary may not be possible for a particular church. Several churches then can come together to support the missionary. The board facilitates communication and cooperation between the churches. Perhaps the most visible function of the board is the handling of financial matters. When a church decides to support a missionary, the church sends funds to the board. All the monies from the supporting churches are collected and sent to the missionary's foreign bank account. The board insures that the funds are converted to the monetary unit of the particular country. Additionally, the board

helps the missionary with taxes, insurance, and legal issues. Many boards assist the missionary with the national government. Passports, visas, and work permits require special attention from folks that have special expertise and experience. One vital service that the board performs for the local church relates to accountability. All believers will give an account of their life and work at the Judgment Seat of Christ. Since the church is the sending or commissioning agency for the missionary, the missionary should be accountable to the church. The board helps prepare reports and enforce standards that the church reviews.

Some Final Thoughts

Let's say that you sign up for basketball in your physical education class next year. The coach brings everyone into the classroom on the first day. He explains the history, rules, strategies and benefits of playing basketball. The following class period, captains choose teams, and the game begins! After forty-five minutes of missed shots, fouls, and general chaos, you are very glad to go to science or math class! What happened? While you and your classmates may know about basketball, much practice and hard work is needed to play well. Missions is exactly the same. You now know some of the basics. In the next chapter, we will explore the opportunities and issues that confront career missionaries. To genuinely understand missions, you now need to begin doing the work of a missionary. Your school may have only one or two basketball courts. God's work today has billions of opportunities waiting for you. Why not pick one of those billions and tell him how he can have eternal life through Jesus Christ?

Developing the Skill

A Christian can be a missionary anywhere, but most Christians never lead another person to Christ. Knowing how to talk to another person about spiritual subjects will often diminish the fear that stops most Christians. Easy methods of witnessing include giving your testimony, passing out tracts, and explaining the Romans Road. Which method would you use with your neighbor that lives across the street? Why?

Review Questions

True or False

____1. God's principles for missions do not apply to modern Christians.

____2. The world's population is over six billion people.

____3. Sin has a positive effect on man's culture.

____4. *Church* refers to a building for meetings.

____5. The church in Antioch sent Paul to preach to the Roman world.

Short Answer

6. Explain various ways people use the term *Christian.*

7. Identify at least three countries in the 10-40 window.

8. What are the "gates of the hell" in Matthew 16?

9. Why did the church establish the office of deacon?

10. How does a mission board help a missionary with money?

Chapter Four

God's Special Servants

4

James and Allen Johnson munched french fries while sitting in the parking lot of a fast food restaurant. The game did not start for another hour, and besides, who could resist the smell of those fries! James heard Allen counting very softly,

"One, two, three, four, wow, five."

"Making sure you get a fair share of the fries?" asked James.

Allen responded, "No, I'm counting red cars out on the highway, and a little sports car just went by!"

James sighed. Just then a new, blue pick-up truck pulled out of the parking lot and headed south. In four minutes, he counted twelve blue cars. Next, the brothers counted white cars, green cars, trucks, motorcycles, and vans. Car watching and fry munching was now the preferred activity before ball games. Once home, the guys said nothing about basketball but could hardly stop talking about all the different types of vehicles on the road. Each had a favorite car. Both would settle for whatever they could afford and what Dad would approve.

The Missionaries' Design

God's servants are similar to the vehicles James and Allen saw on the highway. All are different—in fact, the variety seems endless. But all are the same. The cars have engines, wheels, seats, brakes, and lights. Owners use them to get from one place to the next and for transporting materials. In this chapter, we will survey the differences and similarities in mission work and missionaries. Just as men design and build cars, so God designs and builds His people to work for His glory.

Let's consider some similarities in God's design for all believers. We already know that God created us in His own image. Romans 3:23 records that we fall short of God's glory when we sin. Wrecked cars are not pretty sights and neither are sinful men. Keep in mind the great principle of missions and theology: God wants to fellowship with you and me. The sin problem separated man from God; therefore God sent His Son to die as a substitute for sinners. God's purpose is to recreate man to be like His Son. Jesus told Nicodemus that man must be born again. A child or an adult cannot be born again physically but can be born again spiritually. The new birth is the beginning of a new life with God. Paul tells us, "And be renewed in the spirit of your mind; And that ye put on the new man, which after God is created in righteousness and true holiness" (Eph. 4:23-24). God creates a new person when we accept Christ as Savior. Our job as Christians is to develop that new person in holiness and righteousness. All Christians should therefore be holy and righteous.

God also gives His children special gifts and abilities that make us different. Have you ever wondered why one Christian may teach well while another is better at praying? Some may have great intellectual capacity while others have artistic ability. Consider three significant phases in I Corinthians 12:4-6.

> Now there are *diversities of gifts,* but the same Spirit. And there are *differences of administrations,* but the same Lord. And there are *diversities of operations,* but it is the same God which worketh all in all (emphasis added).

Notice the three members of the Trinity at work regarding spiritual gifts. *Diversities of gifts* simply means that some Christians may have different gifts from others. *Administrations* derives from the same word as *deacon* and means "ministries" or

Seeing the Need

"Expect great things from God. Attempt great things for God."

William Carey (1761-1834) saw something that the religious leaders of his day did not see. While sitting at his cobbler's bench looking at world maps, he realized that the great populations of the world were lost and headed for eternal judgment. "Enlarge the place of thy tent, and let them stretch forth the curtains of thine habitations: spare not, lengthen thy cords, and strengthen thy stakes"(Isa. 54:2). God wanted to save the heathen! God expected the church to take the message of salvation to the heathen! Many ridiculed his vision. Carey preached an eloquent sermon on attempting great things for God and then helped to establish the Particular Baptist Society for Propagating the Gospel among the Heathen. Later, Carey would himself go to India and work for 40 years. He preached, discipled, translated the Bible into several languages, started a college, and initiated social reforms. A statue erected by the government in Serampore, India, honors his life and work. Church historians regard William Carey as the father of modern missions.

What do you see when looking at people around the world?

"service." The idea is that God gives us various places to work. *Operations* sounds a lot like *energy* when pronounced in the original Greek. Turning a switch from off to on energizes a light and makes it useful. God energizes certain efforts at specific times according to His will. Don't let the differences between you and your friends puzzle you. God gave you those abilities. Your task is to develop and use the gifts for the Lord at every opportunity.

The Missionaries' Tasks

God uniquely designs and equips specific people as missionaries. Allen Johnson may see a large truck with a basket attached to a cranelike boom. The signs on the side read, "Power Company." He quickly realizes that the truck belongs to the local electric company and that it's used for repairing power lines. Recognizing the traits and gifts of a missionary may not be so easy. Missionaries work all over the world performing a great variety of tasks. The gifts that make one person suitable for work in tribal areas are much different than those for large cities. Let's first consider a few of the various types of missionaries.

Church Planting

The term "church planting" or "church planter" comes from a common figure of speech in the New Testament to describe the beginning of a new ministry for the Lord. Jesus used the parable of the sower to teach that people receive God's Word differently. Paul well realized that conversion and the establishment of new churches was the work of God and not the work of man: "I have planted, Apollos watered; but God gave the increase. So then neither is he that planteth any thing, neither he that watereth; but God that giveth the increase" (I Cor. 3:6-7). Acts and the Epistles record the beginning, development, and struggles of newly planted churches in the first century.

Countless cities and rural areas across the world do not have a Bible-believing church. Billions of people do not know about Jesus and His power to save them from sin. A church-planting missionary seeks to evangelize an area and begin a local church for the believers. He may begin by passing out tracts, talking to people, and trying to win them to Christ. Services often start with just the missionary's family and grow as people are saved or hear about the meetings. The church planter will teach the new converts how to win others to Christ and how to live as a Christian. Those with leadership potential may be trained to guide the work when the missionary leaves.

Planting a church on the mission field is a great challenge. Communicating spiritual truths to people who speak another language is often the first difficulty encountered by the missionary. Most missionaries spend a lifetime trying to understand the customs and culture of the people. Sometimes the presence of other religions or cults makes the people distrust the missionaries. Each field offers unique challenges. To be used of God, the missionary must adopt Paul's heart: "Therefore I endure all things for the elect's sakes, that they may also obtain the salvation which is in Christ Jesus with eternal glory" (II Tim. 2:10).

Knowing the Culture

"No. You would be killed. They cannot be reached."

Mary Slessor (1848-1913) refused to hear the friends who tried to prevent her from going to a tribe of cannibals in west Africa. This brave Scottish lady was the first white person to live with the Okoyong people and to tell them about Jesus Christ. She soon realized that their preoccupation with drunkenness made them fight and unable to hear the gospel. Mary convinced the men to try trading their yams for cloth and other possessions. As the Okoyong began trading with the outside world, they also began to understand Christianity. Many turned to Christ. Mary Slessor's insight and bravery was the key factor in opening a very difficult place for the spread of the gospel.

What keeps your friends and relatives from accepting Christ?

Tentmaking

No, tentmaking is not a ministry to campers, nor is it a ministry to people who live in tents! Aquila, Priscilla, and Paul made tents to support themselves in Corinth while they preached the gospel and started a church. A modern tentmaker is a person who works in a secular profession in a foreign country and also functions as a missionary. Many governments will not allow a church planter to enter the country. The same government may, however, recognize the need for people with specific skills and professions. A missionary can then work in the country as a teacher or an engineer while spreading the gospel. As people trust Christ and are discipled, the tentmaker begins a church. Since the missionary earns a salary from his work, raising financial support is not required. Vocational excellence is a necessity. The government must realize that the foreigner can do a better job than the national. The special struggles of a tentmaker include being alone without spiritual fellowship in a strange land and having little time for the ministry due to secular work. God is greatly using "vocational missionaries," and many new opportunities open every year.

Bible Teaching

Let's learn a new word—*indigenous* is an adjective that describes the native origin of something. An indigenous plant is one that grows naturally in a place without requiring external intervention. Christian leaders use the term to describe a church that is led and supported by the people who attend it. In other words, missionaries and outside money are not required. The New

Learning the Language

"Get ready, old 'What is this here' is coming down the path."

J. B. Williams, missionary to Benin, West Africa, learned important words in the Bariba language by asking children the simple question, "What is this here?" Bariba is a tonal language and at that time it was unwritten. Williams and his co-workers labored diligently at communicating with the people in their native dialect. On one occasion a visitor from Ireland came, and Rev. Williams began teaching him Bariba. The visitor ran around the room and asked the children, "What is this here?" He announced to his teacher that he had learned the word for "run." J.B. Williams told him that the children really said, "acting like a monkey!"

Why is learning the language of the people so important?

—from *God's Leading Hand* by J. B. Williams, BJUP, p. 18

Testament supports this concept. A missionary may start the church and then turn it over to a national pastor. The issue faced by missionaries is how to train the men who can become national pastors. Teaching the Bible, theology, church administration, and other skills is a full-time job. Many mission fields have the need for dedicated educators attached to schools or Bible institutes. Trained nationals can also assume teaching positions. Missionaries must strive to train the national and work themselves out of a job. They may then move on to another city or need. Teaching the national is then critical to the success of the missionary. Paul told Timothy, "And the things that thou hast heard of me among many witnesses, the same commit thou to faithful men, who shall be able to teach others also" (II Tim. 2:2).

Bible Translating

Much of the English-speaking Christian world takes for granted having a readable copy of the Bible. Most of us own several copies and perhaps several translations. Having the Bible in the native language of the people is key to evangelism and church growth. People numbering into the hundreds of millions still do

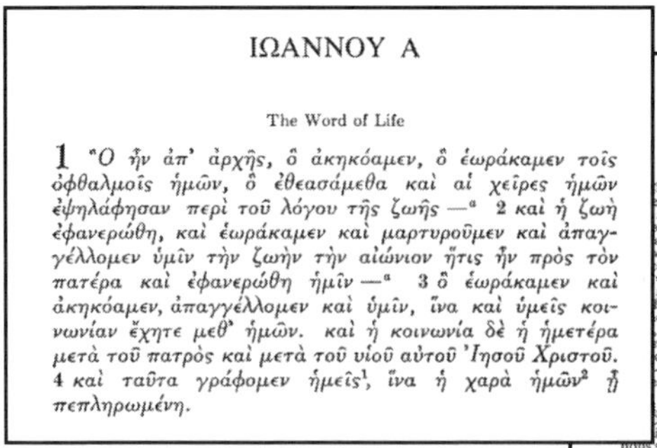

ΙΩΑΝΝΟΥ Α

The Word of Life

1 Ὃ ἦν ἀπ' ἀρχῆς, ὃ ἀκηκόαμεν, ὃ ἑωράκαμεν τοῖς
ὀφθαλμοῖς ἡμῶν, ὃ ἐθεασάμεθα καὶ αἱ χεῖρες ἡμῶν
ἐψηλάφησαν περὶ τοῦ λόγου τῆς ζωῆς —[a] 2 καὶ ἡ ζωὴ
ἐφανερώθη, καὶ ἑωράκαμεν καὶ μαρτυροῦμεν καὶ ἀπαγ-
γέλλομεν ὑμῖν τὴν ζωὴν τὴν αἰώνιον ἥτις ἦν πρὸς τὸν
πατέρα καὶ ἐφανερώθη ἡμῖν —[a] 3 ὃ ἑωράκαμεν καὶ
ἀκηκόαμεν, ἀπαγγέλλομεν καὶ ὑμῖν, ἵνα καὶ ὑμεῖς κοι-
νωνίαν ἔχητε μεθ' ἡμῶν. καὶ ἡ κοινωνία δὲ ἡ ἡμετέρα
μετὰ τοῦ πατρὸς καὶ μετὰ τοῦ υἱοῦ αὐτοῦ Ἰησοῦ Χριστοῦ.
4 καὶ ταῦτα γράφομεν ἡμεῖς[1], ἵνα ἡ χαρὰ ἡμῶν[2] ᾖ
πεπληρωμένη.

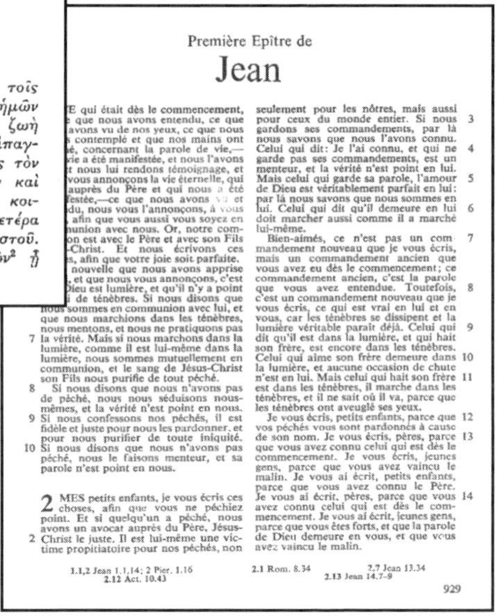

Première Epître de

Jean

E qui était dès le commencement,
que nous avons entendu, ce que
avons vu de nos yeux, ce que nous
contemplé et que nos mains ont
é, concernant la parole de vie,—
vie a été manifestée, et nous l'avons
t nous lui rendons témoignage, et
vous annonçons la vie éternelle, qui
auprès du Père et qui nous a été
festée,—ce que nous avons vu et
du, nous vous l'annonçons, à vous
afin que vous aussi vous soyez en
munion avec nous. Or, notre com-
on est avec le Père et avec son Fils
-Christ. Et nous écrivons ces
s, afin que votre joie soit parfaite.
nouvelle que nous avons apprise
, et que nous vous annonçons, c'est
Dieu est lumière, et qu'il n'y a point
i de ténèbres. Si nous disons que
nous sommes en communion avec lui, et
que nous marchions dans les ténèbres,
nous mentons, et nous ne pratiquons pas
7 la vérité. Mais si nous marchons dans la
lumière, comme il est lui-même dans la
lumière, nous sommes mutuellement en
communion, et le sang de Jésus-Christ
son Fils nous purifie de tout péché.
8 Si nous disons que nous n'avons pas
de péché, nous nous séduisons nous-
mêmes, et la vérité n'est point en nous.
9 Si nous confessons nos péchés, il est
fidèle et juste pour nous les pardonner, et
pour nous purifier de toute iniquité.
10 Si nous disons que nous n'avons pas
péché, nous le faisons menteur, et sa
parole n'est point en nous.

2 MES petits enfants, je vous écris ces
choses, afin que vous ne péchiez
point. Et si quelqu'un a péché, nous
avons un avocat auprès du Père, Jésus-
2 Christ le juste. Il est lui-même une vic-
time propitiatoire pour nos péchés, non
seulement pour les nôtres, mais aussi
pour ceux du monde entier. Si nous 3
gardons ses commandements, par là
nous savons que nous l'avons connu.
Celui qui dit: Je l'ai connu, et qui ne 4
garde pas ses commandements, est un
menteur, et la vérité n'est point en lui.
Mais celui qui garde sa parole, l'amour 5
de Dieu est véritablement parfait en lui:
par là nous savons que nous sommes en
lui. Celui qui dit qu'il demeure en lui 6
doit marcher aussi comme il a marché
lui-même.
Bien-aimés, ce n'est pas un com- 7
mandement nouveau que je vous écris,
mais un commandement ancien que
vous avez eu dès le commencement; ce
commandement ancien, c'est la parole
que vous avez entendue. Toutefois, 8
c'est un commandement nouveau que je
vous écris, ce qui est vrai en lui et en
vous, car les ténèbres se dissipent et la
lumière véritable paraît déjà. Celui qui 9
dit qu'il est dans la lumière, et qui hait
son frère, est encore dans les ténèbres.
Celui qui aime son frère demeure dans 10
la lumière, et aucune occasion de chute
n'est en lui. Mais celui qui hait son frère 11
est dans les ténèbres, il marche dans les
ténèbres, et il ne sait où il va, parce que
les ténèbres ont aveuglé ses yeux.
Je vous écris, petits enfants, parce que 12
vos péchés vous sont pardonnés à cause
de son nom. Je vous écris, pères, parce 13
que vous avez connu celui qui est dès le
commencement. Je vous écris, jeunes
gens, parce que vous avez vaincu le
malin. Je vous ai écrit, petits enfants,
parce que vous avez connu le Père.
Je vous ai écrit, pères, parce que vous 14
avez connu celui qui est dès le com-
mencement. Je vous ai écrit, jeunes gens,
parce que vous êtes forts, et que la parole
de Dieu demeure en vous, et que vous
avez vaincu le malin.

1.1,2 Jean 1.1,14; 2 Pier. 1.16
2.12 Act. 10.43
2.1 Rom. 8.34
2.7 Jean 13.34
2.13 Jean 14.7-9

929

not have any portion of the Word in their language. Bible translation groups indicate work on thousands of projects. Consider the enormity of just one language. A linguist trained in Greek and Hebrew must learn the language of the people. Sometimes, if the language is not written, an alphabet must be invented. The linguist then translates a book,

Spreading the News by Radio

"Radio is the fastest way of reaching the greatest number of people for the least amount of money."

Rolen Cornelius spent 40 years working behind the scenes to spread God's Word by radio. Few people ever saw him. His voice was seldom heard except during an occasional shift at the station's control board. He and his wife Arlene began radio work in Liberia and later moved to the Caribbean island of Antigua. They built the Caribbean Radio Lighthouse, a small AM station that uses mainly Caribbean broadcasters to preach the Word. In the 1990s, they moved to Carriacou, Grenada, and established the Harbour Light of the Windwards radio station. Thousands of people listen regularly to the preaching and music on these stations. Rolen Cornelius loved the Caribbean people and understood how to build and run a radio station for Christ.

Why is the radio ministry an effective means of spreading the Word?

and others check it for accuracy and understandability. Eventually, the work is printed and then shipped back to the country for distribution. The process can take decades. Christian leaders know the power of God's Word and greatly value having it in the native language of the people.

Technical Support

Everyone reading this chapter enjoys the benefits of modern technology. Authors and editors prepared the text, graphic artists used computers to generate the illustrations, and printers used mechanical printing presses to produce your copy of this book. Christian leaders understand the benefits of new inventions for spreading the gospel. Let's consider just a few. Medical missionaries provide care for the sick and injured. As people wait to see the doctor or nurse, an evangelist preaches the Word or hands out gospel literature. The love of Christ is evident for both the body and soul. For hundreds of years, reaching the lost in interior areas required long, dangerous journeys. Today, missionary pilots can land planes almost anywhere. Printers produce Bibles, hymnals, Sunday school materials, and hundreds of other items used in the work. Christian radio stations broadcast the Word to many places without the gospel. Small transistor radios are plentiful around the world. People listen and are challenged to turn to Christ and to grow. Each of these ministries and many more support the primary work of establishing local churches.

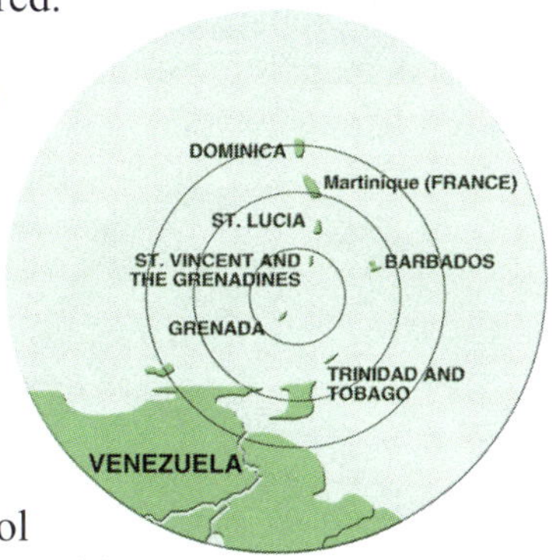

The Missionaries' Cycle

The next time you travel, notice all the types of cars on the road. Remember that God uses a great variety of people and skills on the mission field. He will even use you. Vehicles of all sorts work in specified cycles. The driver starts the car, puts it in gear, presses the accelerator, steers, and brakes. He drives to the destination, puts the car in "park," and turns it off. The next trip follows about the same pattern. Missionaries also have a pattern that we should understand as we try to support the work.

Calling and Training

In Acts 13, the Holy Spirit separated Paul and Barnabas for work as missionary evangelists. God did not ask or direct the entire church to go, just two men and some companions. This selection as missionaries we designate as a "calling." We will look at the specifics of the call to service later in the course. Since Paul was already busy with the work in Antioch, he did not require any additional training. He just packed up and started to preach.

The Lord still calls people to missions today and He expects them to prepare accordingly. Preparation is often very challenging and demanding, but the joy of reaching people for Christ in a foreign land is beyond description. The best things in life require the most work. How many hours would you need to work to buy a car? When you finally have enough money to purchase it, the work and toil seem distant. The satisfaction of being used by God requires diligent preparation for the prospective missionary. He or she needs formal Bible training and perhaps a seminary degree. In some cases, language school follows, as does an internship. God took Moses through forty years of training in Egypt and then forty more in the wilderness to prepare him to lead the Israelites out of slavery. Jesus intensely trained the disciples for three years before sending them into the world. God always prepares His workers.

Deputation

Once the formal training is complete, most prospective missionaries will join a board and begin raising support. They may travel to the field for a short time to learn about the specifics of the work and increase their vision. Once back home, the missionary will contact churches for both prayer and financial support. Much time is spent traveling to various churches and presenting the work. As a greater percentage of support is promised, the missionary will begin making final preparations to go to the field. The specific preparations will depend upon the location of the field and the type of ministry. All will need medical checkups, visas, passports, equipment, travel arrangements, and more. Deputation can be difficult, but the Lord does supply strength, and He uses the time to further prepare the missionary for service.

The Field

Traveling to the field a hundred years ago could take weeks or months. Today, most missionaries board a plane and arrive at the field in hours. Often, a veteran missionary will meet the newcomers and help them to adjust to the new location and culture. Most boards advise staying on the field for about four years before returning home. Others prefer about two years, depending upon the work. Settling into a new house, speaking a new language, learning how to buy food, recognizing which insects to avoid, and adapting to the weather may take months. As nationals see the missionary learning and sometimes struggling, many will comprehend the love of Christ. As living in a foreign land becomes easier, missionaries begin the work. Some missionaries report that the second four-year term on the field is much more productive than the first because they know how things work.

Furlough

Furlough is the time when a missionary returns home to rest and report to supporting churches on the work. Seeing the relatives and eating at a favorite restaurant can be very exciting for those who have been away for a long time.

Missionaries enjoy the fellowship with their sending church. Most pastors are very glad to have them in the church as examples to the congregation. Some may need medical attention not available on the field. Others will seek additional training. Much time is spent speaking to churches and schools, encouraging more participation in the work. Furloughs may last a year, though the trend seems to be toward shorter ones. Then the missionary family departs for the field and the cycle begins again!

Conclusion

Most of us take very good care of our cars. We need them to travel back and forth to school or work. If the car breaks down, life is in turmoil! God likewise takes very good care of His servants. The message of the cross must be preached around the world. Let's be very honest. God's call to the mission field may be very difficult to obey. Some reject His will for an easier life at home. Others understand the greatness of God's ability to sustain them and understand, too, the terrible condition of the lost. Men may look at us as small, broken-down vehicles. God may look at us and see the means to influence thousands for Christ. God may not call you to go, but you should be willing and moldable.

David Livingstone heard his future father-in-law, Robert Moffat, say, "I have sometimes seen, in the morning sun, the smoke of a thousand villages where no missionary has ever been." These words inspired Livingstone to spend his life evangelizing and exploring Africa. Livingstone's poem shows us his heart. The "anywhere" was Africa in the 1800s.

Lord, Send Me Anywhere

O Lord, since Thou hast died to give Thyself for me,
No sacrifice could be too great for me to make for Thee.

I only have one life, and that will soon be past;
I want my life to count for Christ, what's done for Him will last.

I follow Thee, my Lord, and glory in Thy cross;
I gladly leave the world behind and count all gain as loss.

Lord, send me anywhere, only go with me;
Lay any burden on me, only sustain me.
Sever any tie, save the tie that binds me to Thy heart,
Lord Jesus, my King, I consecrate my life, Lord, to Thee.

Review Questions

Short Answer

1. What two characteristics should be true of all Christians?

2. What is the Christian's responsibility concerning spiritual gifts?

3. Name at least two difficulties encountered by missionary church planters.

4. What word is applied to a church whose support and leadership come from the local people?

5. Name at least three languages that a translator must know in order to translate the Bible effectively.

6. What training does a missionary require?

7. What does a missionary do on furlough?

8. Who developed a burden for missions while reading a secular book?

9. Who wrote the poem, "Lord, Send Me Anywhere"?

10. Who was Paul's preaching companion in Acts 13?

CHAPTER FIVE

Supporting the Troops

5

Life could hardly be better for Jason Moore. School was out. He had actually made the honor roll, and Dad was telling everyone about it. The first big activity for the summer meant traveling to Uncle Jack's farm in the country for the ten-year family reunion. Jason well remembered the last one. The best part was listening to Grandfather and several uncles tell stories about fighting in World War II, Korea, and Vietnam. Cousin Ron would be at this reunion. Last time, he had been in Saudi Arabia with the Marines and would no doubt join in the conversation with stories about the Gulf War.

"Tell us about driving tanks and shooting off missiles," Jason shouted as Ron sat down under the shade tree. The older Moore military veterans soon gathered and obviously wanted a good war story. Ron promptly displayed a commendation medal from his commanding general. The family squawked approvingly.

"I didn't see one missile in the desert and hardly saw any tanks. I ran the division's water plant," Ron said proudly.

Grandfather almost choked on his lemonade and finally muttered something about family tradition and honor.

Ron gathered his composure after sensing the family's bewilderment. He told them about the medal ceremony. The general had pointed out that the war's three key components included fuel, ammunition, and water. Five hundred thousand soldiers and officers required lots of water in the hot desert. Ron had worked night and day to make drinking water from the sea. He had even repaired the water unit by using parts from a broken-down jeep.

"Soldier, your dedication to the water plant kept us going. This division could not survive in this heat without you. The nation will remember us for bravery and victory. We will remember and honor you for faithfully supporting us."

Grandfather smiled. Ron would never forget the general's words. Ron understood that the unseen people behind the front lines are just as important as the heroes who get most of the attention.

According to military experts, nine support personnel stand behind every soldier on the battlefield. God's army is much the same. Christians honor the work of missionaries, and rightly so. Missionaries could never reach the lost and establish churches without faithful supporters at home. In this chapter we will look at ways you can assist missionaries. The new believer won to Christ by a missionary in Peru may not know your name or anything about you. But God knows that you had a big part in that person's conversion. Supporting missions is a great calling!

Bible Basics

Have you ever thought that in the next few years, you will begin to lead God's work on the earth? Leadership can be frightening, but God prepares us for every step. Right now, you should be learning basic Bible principles for living and working. In time, God will test you in many ways to prove and to develop your integrity. As people see your good character, they will begin to give you additional responsibilities. The cycle will repeat many times. The key to spiritual progress and leadership is how well you apply the Bible to life. We learned earlier in the course that the Lord takes great interest in missions. Let's examine a few passages that should guide our actions about missionary support.

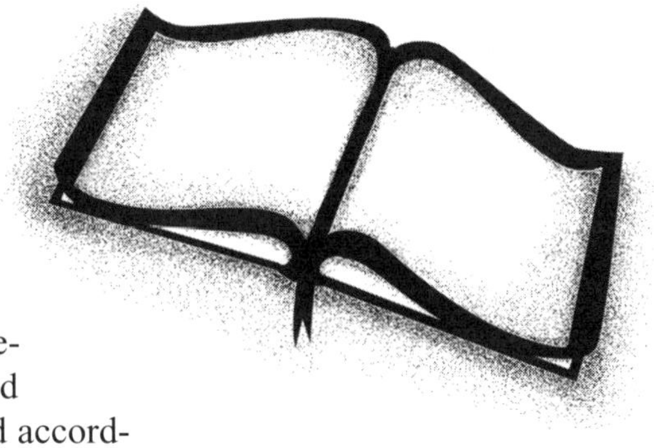

In the Garden of Eden, Satan tempted Eve by diverting her attention from God's goodness and by focusing it upon herself. She believed that God withheld good things from her and she acted accordingly. "Me first" is today one of the driving forces of humanity. God designed something far better for believers. The apostle Paul knew that selfish actions caused divisions in the Philippian church. He wrote,

> Fulfil ye my joy, that ye be likeminded, having the same love, being of one accord, of one mind. Let nothing be done through strife or vainglory; but in lowliness of mind let each esteem other better than themselves. Look not every man on his own things, but every man also on the things of others. Let this mind be in you, which was also in Christ Jesus (Phil. 2:2-5).

Believers focus on the needs of others just as Christ focused on our needs when He died for sin. The application to missions is simple. We need to concentrate on the spiritual needs of the lost and not on earthly things that pertain to us. Missionaries dedicate themselves completely to the needs of others. Believers like you and I should be willing to give at least some of our time and energy to the lost. Missions provides many opportunities.

First Samuel 30 provides us with the principle of shared reward. David and 600 men conducted a military rescue operation to reclaim their families and possessions. He left 200 men behind at a brook due to their exhaustion. Some time later, David and the 400 soldiers returned victoriously. David decided to give each person an equal share of the spoils. He said, "But as his part is that goeth down to the battle, so shall his part be that tarrieth by the stuff: they shall part alike" (I Sam. 30:24). This concept guided Israel's war policy for hundreds of years and should greatly encourage us today. We may not travel to foreign lands to win the lost and start churches. But if we actively support the missionaries who do, we will share in the reward!

In Matthew 10 Christ instructs His disciples on preaching the gospel. His concluding comments (vv. 40-42) discuss people who assist those who preach. Notice that even the smallest act of kindness and support receives God's attention and commendation. "And whosoever shall give to drink unto one of these little ones a cup of cold water only in the name of a disciple, verily I say unto you, he shall in no wise lose his reward" (Matt. 10:42). Imagine God's pleasure and our reward for undertaking larger support projects!

Homework

Smart military commanders know both their own troops and the things they may face in battle. Careful planning ensures the most efficient use of resources to achieve the objective. Christians must know the missionaries and their particular needs in order to provide effective support. We learned that missionaries do not come in one-size-fits-all packaging. Each ministry is unique. Learning about the missionary and his ministry is the first step toward aiding him well. Most boards require their people to send regular prayer letters to supporting churches. Reading several of these letters from the same missionary should begin to help you understand the work. You might also ask the missionary questions via the postal system or e-mail. Libraries and the Internet will furnish much information about the culture of the country. Whenever a missionary is home on furlough or on deputation, ask him to come to class or invite him to a meal. The conversation is fun and will help you to understand that missionaries are just people serving the Lord in different places.

Repeated contact over several months or years will produce solid friendships that all will appreciate. Your new friend will tell you about joys and struggles not mentioned in formal reports and prayer letters.

One challenge faced by the majority of missionaries is the time required living in a foreign culture. We are most efficient when we know how things work. Remember when new students came to your school? They spent a lot of time asking questions, learning names, and trying to understand what was going on. The whole process is very stressful for most. Now multiply that stress by one hundred times for a missionary living in another country, and you will begin to understand the challenge. Something as simple as buying food for the day could involve finding the right market, learning the word for "bread," and figuring out how much to pay for it. Some places even have customs for how to carry food back to the home. The result is that the routine activities of life take time away from ministry. We all have only twenty-four hours in a day, and we need to sleep! Our job as supporters and helpers is to find ways to make the missionary's life more efficient so that more time may be spent in the work. Let's examine a few of the things that we can do here for missions.

Prayer

Paul continually asked believers to pray for him. He understood the connection between the power of God and prayer. Five

The Power of Prayer

". . . to learn to move man, through God, by prayer alone."

Hudson Taylor (1832-1905) started the China Inland Mission in 1865. Early in life, he knew that God wanted him to go to China. Taylor prepared as a doctor and finally departed from England in 1853. Years passed with few results but much hardship. By 1900 when Taylor retired, the mission had grown to 750 missionaries with financial support of about four million dollars. The work established hundreds of mission stations with scores of nationals spreading the gospel. Taylor never appealed to men for money. Rather, he took the need to God through prayer and God answered mightily. One man who learned to pray and to trust God saw perhaps millions saved.

What will your prayers do?

minutes of work blessed by God is more effective than months of hard labor using human wisdom. Faithful missionaries want people to pray for them regularly. Reading prayer letters and corresponding with the missionary will inform you of many specific prayer needs. Let the folks on the field know that you are praying for them. The encouragement will help them face the challenges of the day and will create in them the expectation of God's blessing. Many people place missionary prayer cards on the refrigerator or in their Bibles as a reminder to pray. Keep in mind that prayer is hard work and requires faithfulness. William Carey, the father of modern missions, proclaimed, "I will go to India. I will go, but you at home must hold the ropes." The "rope" of prayer keeps God's servants straight and tall for the work of spreading the Word.

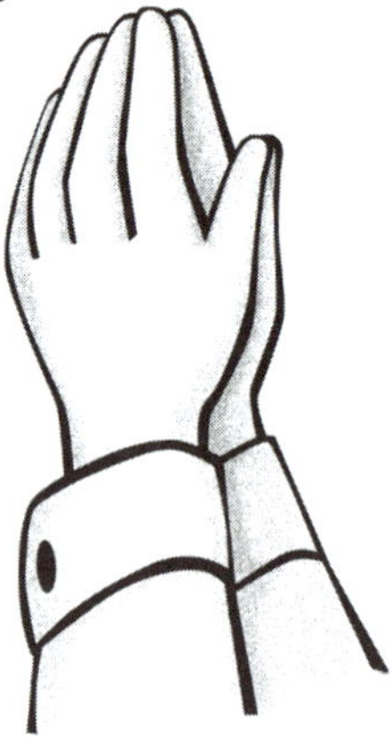

Money

Missionaries need money to live just like you and I do. A very simple way to support missions is to contribute money through

your local church or mission board. As a teen, you should begin giving at least ten percent of any earnings to the Lord's work. You should also consider giving to a specific missionary on a regular basis. Let's focus on the MK's (missionary kid) situation. Most do not have the opportunity to earn money in a foreign country due to work restrictions. Sending a few dollars designated to a teen on the mission field will enable them to buy birthday presents for family members and other personal items. Your thoughtfulness will be remembered and appreciated for a very long time.

School

Missionaries spend much time educating their children. Many use some form of home school, or they work with others to form small Christian schools. Christian textbooks and supplies seldom exist on the field. You could assist by helping to purchase and to ship needed materials. Many MKs surpass their teacher's

---

Pressing for the Mark

"Climb or die."

Isobel Kuhn (1901-57) spent most of her life in western China working among tribal people. Following World War II and the establishment of the communist government, she fled to Burma and eventually to the United States. Her husband John joined her after surveying Thailand for the mission. She was tired and looked forward to quiet years with her family. John believed God wanted them in Thailand. Isobel read a missionary story with pictures of mountains and the caption, "Climb or die." Mountain climbing requires progress or results in death. She knew that the same was true of spiritual life. John and Isobel spent the next two years working with the tribal people of northern Thailand.

Are you climbing spiritual mountains or falling into a valley?

knowledge and experience in upper level courses like math and science. Using e-mail, you could help an MK with homework and projects. Your class or family could adopt a mission school and help with whatever it needs. The effort will further the education of the student and will also give the missionary more time to work with the nationals.

Going to the Field

Praying, communicating, and assisting in various needs produces a great relationship between you and the missionary on the field. A letter or an e-mail brings much excitement as you find out how things are going. Before long, your missionary friend may invite you and a group from your school or church for a visit. Perhaps the ministry needs specific help with a project. The usual reaction to such a request is to decline the invitation. You might reason that such a trip is too expensive or that you do not have the time. Your pastor or teacher probably views the situation differently. Spiritual leaders recognize that the Lord uses trips to the mission field to equip believers for a lifetime of service. Going to the mission field for a couple of weeks does not mean that you will become a career missionary. It does give the Lord the opportunity to teach you things about ministering to different cultures and about living by faith. Your friendship with the missionary will flourish as you see life from a very different perspective. God's work on the mission field will move forward. Let's examine a step-by-step approach to participating in a short-term missions team.

Choosing the Right Opportunity

A missionary must need and want your help for a team to be successful. Some teams believe that mission trips are for a vacation in an exotic land or for sightseeing. Successful missions trips must have a specific ministry-related purpose. Every team should include some type of evangelism. Other typical projects include running vacation Bible schools, participating in camp programs, providing special music, constructing buildings, and assisting with educational needs. The opportunities are as varied as the missionary's ministries and needs. Keep in mind that not every opportunity may be appropriate for you and your group. The potential team members must possess the skills and abilities to do the work. Someone without musical training may not contribute effectively to a music team. Language may also limit some trips. Language may also open opportunities. The Spanish class could go to a Spanish-speaking nation and greatly aid the work. The key to choosing the right trip is knowing the missionaries and their expectations. A team should always seek to help and encourage. "Look not every man on his own things, but every man also on the things of others" (Phil. 2:4).

Planning the Trip

Once the missionary and team leader firmly establish the place and purpose, planning the trip is very exciting! It can also be a lot of work. The process is similar to purchasing a new outfit for a special event. Everything must coordinate and be within a specified budget. It must also be available for purchase. That perfect pair of shoes may be too expensive or may not fit you. Your goal is to make everything work together for the occasion. Four major issues that every team faces include the dates for the trip, travel plans, accommodations on the field, and the cost. Often these issues affect each other. Travel costs may be less expensive if you stay longer on the field, but staying longer requires more money for field accommodations. Careful research and compromise are keys to successful planning. The missionary may be able to provide important information about previous trips.

Each team member must also take specific steps to prepare. You must know what is expected from you as you travel and as

you participate in the work. The group may have training sessions for the ministry on the field. Raising the funds for the trip may be a new experience. Missionaries believe that God pays for those things that are in His will. Team members will rejoice as they see the needs supplied. Passports, visas, and vaccinations may be needed, depending upon the country. Find out how much luggage is acceptable and what is appropriate to take. List all requirements and include medications and other personal care items. The most important personal preparation is to pray for God's power and blessing upon your effort. Going to the mission field can be frightening at first. Prayer will fortify your faith and assure you of God's leading.

Doing the Work

The sights, sounds, and smells of your first few minutes in another country will last in your memory for a lifetime. Being with your missionary friends is exciting! Always ask the missionary to give you an orientation for the location. Obeying tips such as

Mission Teams

"My expectations have definitely been met."

Short-term mission trips aim at helping missionaries and reaching the lost for Christ. In addition, the team members' lives are often changed by the experience.

- "It seems like God just spent this summer teaching me about myself."
- "The Lord taught me a lot about trusting in Him for everything."
- "When I see true servanthood practiced in the lives of these pastors and their wives, I am rebuked."
- "The Lord can use an inexperienced yet willing vessel."

"Stay away from little black and red bugs" or "Use sunscreen" may make life more pleasant for you. The missionary will probably instruct you about the place in which you are staying and about the work. Listening and following instructions are very important. Most teams will establish a pattern for the day's activities. Rest is a vital element. The Lord will be well pleased as you work hard at accomplishing the objective of the trip. Sometimes things don't work out as planned, so flexibility is also important. Try to learn everything possible about the missionary and the people. Your presence can be a big encouragement to all. Trying national foods can be fun. Most trips will also include time for sightseeing and shopping. Souvenirs and pictures will help you remember all the lessons that God is teaching you. At the end of your trip, let the missionary know how God used the experience in your life and assure him of your continued support.

Reporting on the Work

On many occasions the apostle Paul reported on the work to his supporters. Parents will be praying for you as you prepare and go on the trip. Others will contribute financially or will help in other ways. The school, church, or mission board is vitally interested in you and in the work. Each wants and deserves a report on your efforts. Financial accountability may be required. Most teens will talk continually about the trip. Sometimes reporting to a group of people may be harder. Simply prepare well and speak to them as you would to a friend. Using pictures or other items from the country will help. Those who supported you will be greatly encouraged as you share experiences and spiritual lessons. You may even motivate others to participate in the future. Planning the next trip often begins when you report on the first one!

Tail to Tooth

Military recruits enter boot camp to learn how to be soldiers. Every recruit works on the basics of physical fitness, target practice, and following orders. Only about one in ten ever goes into the "tooth," or combat position. The majority work in the "tail," which provides logistical support. As Christians we can work in both the "Tail and Tooth" of God's army, reaching the lost around the world. Missionaries depend upon people like you for help. Age is not a factor in prayer or going to the field. Soldiers in the "tail" may not receive much attention, especially in time of peace. But the officers know what they do and depend upon them for success. God likewise recognizes those who aid the cause by supporting missionaries. His commendation will read, "Well done, thou good and faithful servant" (Matt. 25:21).

Review Questions

Short Answer

1. How should someone prepare to be a Christian leader?

2. Who started the concept of shared reward?

3. Identify several ways to communicate with missionaries.

4. How much money should a teen give to the Lord's work?

5. What is the main purpose of a mission trip?

6. What factors determine the work on a missions trip?

7. What are the four major issues confronted by a team during the planning process?

8. What helps team members remember the field?

9. To whom will you give a report about the team?

10. Who ultimately rewards people for supporting missions?

CHAPTER SIX

Who, Me?

6

Lance Martin sat on the bench and wondered what it would take to win this game. In the last ten minutes, two shots hit the crossbar of the goal. The score was tied. The championship seemed so close. His mind wandered back to the first day of tryouts in October. Coach Collins had clearly told him that as a sophomore he would spend more time watching than playing.

"Perfect your skills this year, particularly that right hook shot, and you will get plenty of field time next year."

Lance worked hard at getting in better physical condition and at shooting from about forty feet. Everyone noticed his determination.

Just then the whistle blew for an injury timeout. Coach ran down the sideline and told Lance to go in as left wing and try the hook shot. Lance sat still.

Tyler Andrews elbowed Lance in the ribs and shouted, "Get in there!"

"Me?" Lance whispered.

Coach Collins' gestures removed all doubt. Lance ran into the game just as the whistle blew to start. With about three minutes remaining, the striker passed the ball to Lance in a crowd of defenders. The ball glanced off a shin guard into an opening. Lance quickly planted his left foot and kicked with everything he had.

The ball started wide of the goal and then hooked back into the net. Victory screams filled the air!

Coach put his arm around Lance and confided, "When you didn't respond to me, I almost put someone else in the game. I knew you could do it given the chance. Good job!"

Almost every person serving God asks the "me?" question at a pivotal time in life. God plans something important for us and begins showing us His will. Some sit in silence just like Lance at the soccer game. Others argue with God. Remember what Moses said? "Who am I, that I should go unto Pharaoh?" Some run like Jonah. Some, like Isaiah, respond immediately.

God wants every believer to spread the gospel and to work in missions. The Great Commission applies to Christians of all generations. Doing God's will is almost contagious. The more you do and see God working, the more you want to work. Some teens will at this point begin to think that God is calling them into full-time service or missions. He indeed may be. A missionary is simply a person that gives all his time to the work and receives some type of financial support. In this final chapter, we will examine the call to full-time service as well as what to do next. The principles apply to all believers.

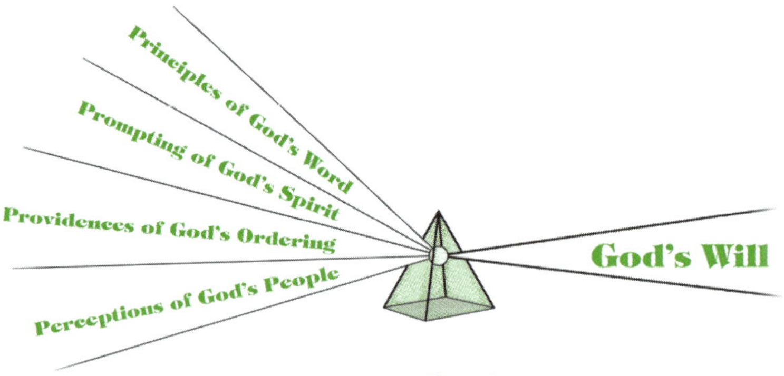

Discerning God's Will

This illustration is based on a reference to "The Sunday School Times" in *The Preacher and His Preaching* by Alfred Gibbs, pg. 89.

Called to Serve

Bob Jones Sr. said, "Success is finding the will of God and doing it." Many teens struggle with God's will. After all, determining what to do with your life is one of the biggest decisions that you will ever make. Spiritual men through the ages generally agree that God's will is knowable but sometimes difficult to discern at first. An older person can look back through many years of life and clearly see God's leading. But for a younger person, looking ahead through the years can be frightening and uncertain. Let's briefly examine four aspects of how to know God's calling for your life.

Consecration

Consecration is a big word that simply means you devote yourself completely to God. Remember that Coach Collins told Lance to work on his basic soccer skills. You may want to take trigonometry next year, but school policy says that you must take algebra as a prerequisite. Likewise, God will show you His will for the future when you start doing the basics and prerequisites today. Moses explained complete devotion as "Hear, O Israel: The Lord our God is one Lord: And thou shalt love the Lord thy God with all thine heart, and with all thy soul, and with all thy might"

Isaiah: Saw God's Glory

Uzziah, one of the most stable kings of Judah, died and left his faithful advisor, **Isaiah**, in turmoil. God then revealed His glory to Isaiah and the cares of earth faded into nothingness. Isaiah was never the same. "Here am I; send me" signaled the beginning of a ministry that would face sorrow, disappointment, and rejection. Through all the difficulties, Isaiah preached the glory of the coming Messiah to the extent that many today herald the book of Isaiah as the fifth gospel. Isaiah's vision changed his understanding of God. He referred to God as the "Holy One of Israel" twenty-five times. "Holy, holy, holy" made a great impact on the man and his message.

Missionaries must clearly see the glory of God to be effective in reaching the lost and in doing God's work. How can you see the glory of God today? How might it change your life?

(Deut. 6:4-5). Believers must know God's unique greatness and then love him wholeheartedly. When we love someone, we choose that person over everybody else. The bride and groom say, "I do," and therefore commit themselves to one another to the exclusion of other people. Loving God means that we focus upon and obey Him as a matter of choice. If God says it, I do it. If my friends want to do something contrary to God, I don't do it. We learn God's ways from reading and studying the Bible. The first step in knowing God's will for life is to do God's will in everything today.

Desire

C. H. Spurgeon wisely told his ministerial class, "If any student in this room could be content to be a newspaper editor, or a grocer, or a farmer, or a doctor, or a lawyer, or a senator, or a king, in the name of heaven and earth let him go his way." A man or woman called into missions will have a great desire to do the work of missions to the exclusion of other things. Keep in mind that most believers are not called into full-time Christian work. God may want you to be a teacher and if so, He will give you a love for teaching. Missionaries spend many years preparing for the field and some endure great hardship. The burning desire to take the gospel to the lost sustains them through the years. God wants His people to be happy and content. The words *rejoice* and *joy* occur over 350 times in the Bible. Imagine the misery of working for a lifetime in an occupation that you despised. God does not want you to be miserable. If He is calling you into missions, He will give you the desire to be a missionary.

Leading

Perhaps one of the most amazing characteristics of God is His ability to arrange circumstances to accomplish His will. In Genesis, Joseph had no thoughts or ambitions to become the prime minister of Egypt. God providentially ordered the affairs of his life and then equipped him with special gifts. Joseph performed God's will every day and eventually became a very powerful man. Joseph told his brothers, "But as for you, ye thought evil against me; but God meant it unto good, to bring to pass, as it is this day, to save much people alive" (Gen. 50:20). God works through circumstances that we may not understand to bring us to the place and work of His choosing.

God will order your affairs so that you will be able to discern your life's work. If He wants you to be a missionary, He will give you the right gifts and opportunities. The particular set of circumstances will be different for every person. You must stay in close fellowship with God to perceive His leading in your life.

Approval

The apostle Paul gives us a list of qualifications for ministers in I Timothy 3. The church then uses the list to judge whether or not a man is called into the ministry. Proverbs 11:14 reads, "Where no counsel is, the people fall: but in the multitude of counselors there is safety." Godly people can and should provide you with good advice about your gifts and calling. If God is calling you to be a missionary or into another full-time ministry, the evidence will be clear to other believers. Your parents also will guide you.

The Next Steps

Most of us have played with acorns. They make great ammunition for slingshots! No one argues with the fact that a small acorn can in time and under the right circumstances grow into a huge oak tree. The outward appearance and size are so very different. Genetic material deposited first in the acorn guides the plant through various stages that result in a mature tree. The tree produces acorns, and the cycle begins again.

Teens and acorns have much in common. The unseen material inside guides development. Considerable time passes before bearing fruit. As you contemplate and seek God's will for your life, remember that what you are today may be vastly different than the final product. After totally dedicating yourself to the Lord, follow the godly desires of your heart. God will use His providential leading and the counsel of others to direct you to the next step. If you are not sure about the next step, always give God the benefit of the doubt. Missions and full-time ministries are close to God's heart. Start moving toward Christian service. If God wants you to do otherwise, He

will show you. The lessons learned and time spent will always be useful as a layman in the church. Also, when fear and anxiety about the future trouble you, spend extra time in the Word of God and in prayer. Remember the promises of God! "The steps of a good man are ordered by the Lord: and he delighteth in his way" (Ps. 37:23).

Be a Missionary Today

If you have even the smallest inclination toward missions, there are several things you can do to take the next step. The world is full of people who need to hear about the love of God in Jesus Christ. Start witnessing. Perhaps you could go on the church visitation program. Ask your pastor or principal for suggestions. Look for opportunities to preach and teach. Most churches would welcome help in the Sunday school or bus ministry. Your first attempt at speaking may not turn out well. Most famous preachers and full-time workers through the ages could look back at early failures. A good

Moses: Educated for Service

God used **Moses** to deliver Israel from Egyptian slavery and to write the first five books of the Bible. Moses' life literally shaped the course of human history. Great works require great education. God planned Moses' education to prepare him for future service. Look up the following verses and determine who taught Moses and what he may have learned.

Exodus 2:9
Exodus 2:10
Exodus 2:15-25
Exodus 3:1–6:30

What must you learn to prepare for God's calling upon your life?

Bezaleel: Using God's Gifts

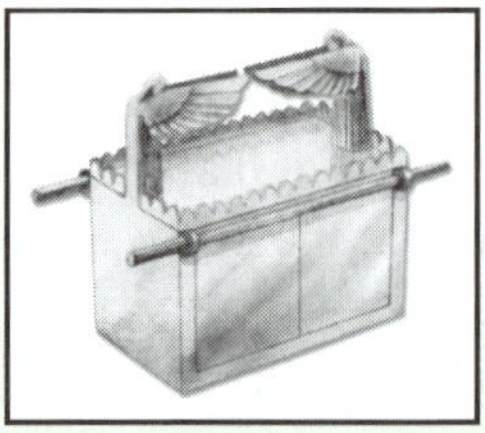

Not all of God's great servants are missionaries or preachers. Some, like **Bezaleel,** are craftsmen who use God's talents to accomplish a great supporting work. Moses praised these men for doing a great job (Exodus 39:43). God's glory then filled the tabernacle, which was an indication of His approval upon the work. Read the following verses and identify all the skills this man used to build the tabernacle and associated items under the direction of Moses.

Exodus 31:1-11; 35:34

What talents do you have that could be used to serve God on the mission field?

way to start is to give your testimony. God may be calling you into a technical support role on the mission field. Learn all you can about that technical field. Ask for help and information from those currently working in the vocation. Faithful men of God always work and move with a sense of urgency. Develop zeal for the things of God.

Get an Education

The next time you go to a doctor or dentist, ask about his education. Government agencies require years of formal, intensive education before granting certification as a medical professional. Doctors must also attend a set number of classes each year.

Missionaries deal with men's souls that will live forever. Formal training is therefore vitally important. Most mission boards require at least a bachelor's degree and many prefer seminary or graduate training. Remember that missionaries deal with many subjects including foreign languages, anthropology, theology, and Scripture. Veteran missionaries will encourage you to get every bit of academic training that you possibly can.

Choose a school with a reputation for spiritual vitality and academic excellence. Your pastor or other spiritual leaders can guide you. Evaluate the graduates of various schools and determine which school produces the best-qualified missionaries. Mission boards may also provide suggestions.

Support Missions

The earlier chapters of this book contain many ways to support missions and missionaries. Select a ministry and volunteer to do anything that is needed. In most cases, the missionary will respond positively and your relationship will flourish. Participate in one short-term team every year. Try to go to different places. The Lord will teach you to live by faith as you see life from a missionary perspective. In Acts 13, Paul and Barnabas actively taught the church at Antioch. The Holy Spirit then clearly led the men to start the first missionary journey. Like Paul and Barnabas, you should be as active in God's work today as possible. God will open doors of opportunity and blessing.

C. T. Studd: Reflecting on a Life Given to God's Service

C. T. Studd (1862-1931) lived with great passion for God. His work touched China, India, and Africa. Nearing death, he gave very encouraging advice to an African evangelist going to reach hostile tribes.

"My time is nearly finished among you black people. I only go on from day to day as God gives me strength. So don't depend upon me, depend upon God; He is with you, He won't die, He will keep you.

"Don't go with shame! Don't be afraid! Be bold and preach the gospel! Don't drag the flag of God in the earth! Put it up and don't bring shame upon it. Set your face like a soldier to overcome."

Norman Grubb, *C.T. Studd: Cricketer and Pioneer* (Harrisburg, PA: Evangelical Press, 1935), 241.

Blazing Hearts

Missions is an exciting calling and is perhaps the greatest of all works. God wants every man, woman, and child to know Jesus Christ. Peter tells us that God is "not willing that any should perish, but that all should come to repentance" (II Pet. 3:9). All Christians must participate in the business of saving souls from destruction. William Carey said, "My business is preaching the gospel, and I cobble shoes to pay the expenses." Your calling may be into a secular workplace. Always remember that your real job is to witness for Christ and to support missionaries around the world.

God will call some into full-time missionary service. David Brainerd, a missionary to native Americans in the 1700s, wrote, "As long as I see anything to be done for God, life is worth having; but O how vain and unworthy it is to live for any lower end." This man zealously pursued the souls of the lost and the encouragement of believers until his dying day. God used him to mold a generation of God's servants. May we likewise pursue the work of God with all of our hearts!

Review Exercises

Short Answer

1. How does a missionary differ from a typical Christian?

2. What is the meaning of consecration?

3. Where is the Bible's list of qualifications for a minister?

4. What must all believers do for God?

5. Name three things you can do for missions today.

6. Why should believers not worry about the future and God's will?

Matching

A. Taught by father-in-law

B. Built the tabernacle

C. Preached in Africa

D. Saw God's throne

E. Made shoes

____ 7. William Carey

____ 8. Moses

____ 9. Bezaleel

____ 10. Isaiah

Photograph Credits

The following agencies and individuals have furnished materials to meet the photographic needs of this textbook. We wish to express our gratitude to them for their important contribution.

American Tract Society
The Bob Jones University Collection
Christian Literature Crusade
Corel Corporation
Doug Garland
Geremy Butler Photography
Paul Gillette
Good News Publishers
Joyce Landis
Library of Congress
Joy McCarnan
Mexican Government Tourism Office
Overseas Missionary Fellowship
PhotoDisc, Inc.
United Bible Society
Unusual Films
J. B. Williams

Chapter 1

Doug Garland 3; *Isaiah's Lips Anointed by Fire* by Pietro Negroni, The Bob Jones University Collection, photo by Unusual Films 6

Chapter 3

Corel Corporation 28, 29; Paul Gillette 30; Unusual Films 33

Chapter 4

Unusual Films 42; J. B. Williams 43 (top); Doug Garland 43, 44 (bottom); used with permission from United Bible Society 44 (top left); used with permission from Joy McCarnan 44 (top right); Corel Corporation 47; Library of Congress 49

Chapter 5

Corel Corporation 56; Mexican Government Tourism Office 57; Overseas Missionary Fellowship 58; Geremy Butler Photography 59; Unusual Films 59 (top), 63; Joyce Landis 61 (both); PhotoDisc, Inc. 62

Chapter 6

Moses and Aaron Before Pharaoh by Benjamin West, The Bob Jones University Collection, photo by Unusual Films 70 (top), 73 (bottom); Joyce Landis 70 (bottom); American Tract Society 73 (top left, top right, bottom right); Tracts used by permission of Good News Publishers, Wheaton, IL 73 (top, center, left, bottom); Unusual Films 74; Photo of C.T. Studd used with permission from Christian Literature Crusade 75